THE USBORNE
BIG BOOK OF BIG
BUGS

Written by Emily Bone
Illustrated by Fabiano Fiorin

Designed by Stephen Wright
Bugs expert: Dr. Naomi Ewald

Series designer: Laura Wood
Series editor: Jane Chisholm
Additional design: Emily Barden and Helen Edmonds
Image manipulation: John Russell

How big is BIG?

There are millions of different bugs. Lots of them are very small, but others are HUGE. The bugs in this book are shown about the same size as they are in real life.

Some big bugs use their bodies to scare away attackers. The **giant jungle nymph** stands up on its front legs and thrashes its body around.

The **giant huntsman spider** is the BIGGEST SPIDER in the world.

It lays some of the largest eggs of any insect.

The **Saint Helena giant earwig** is about eight times bigger than a common earwig.

Common earwig

Wonderful wings

Flying bugs have thin wings that they flap very quickly to stay up in the air. They use them to reach food and fly away from danger.

Giant mydas flies look like giant wasps, so other bugs don't eat them.

Moths use their feathery antennae (feelers) to find partners.

The **atlas moth** is the BIGGEST FLYING BUG in the world.

Hercules caterpillars are covered in poisonous spikes.

When a **giant bush cricket** flies, its wings look like big leaves. This hides it from potential attackers.

West African antlions have long, speckled wings. This makes it difficult for attackers to spot them in the dry, brown grassland where they live.

The **white witch moth** has the LONGEST WINGS of any bug. When fully open, they would stretch from the top to the bottom of this page.

The bigger a giant dobsonfly's jaws, the more likely he is to attract a female.

Lots of legs

All bugs have at least six legs, but some have lots more. They help them run fast, climb and hunt for food.

The **rhinoceros cockroach** has spiky legs to dig burrows into hard ground.

While it's hiding in the undergrowth, a **Mexican redknee tarantula** can sense whether there is another spider, or something good to eat, walking past.

An **emperor scorpion** uses its big claws to grab and crush prey.

It carries its babies to keep them safe.

These aren't actually legs. They're feelers used to sense food.

Queen Alexandra's caterpillars have bright red and yellow markings. This warns other creatures that they're poisonous.

Giant dobsonflies have a wingspan of over 20cm (8in).

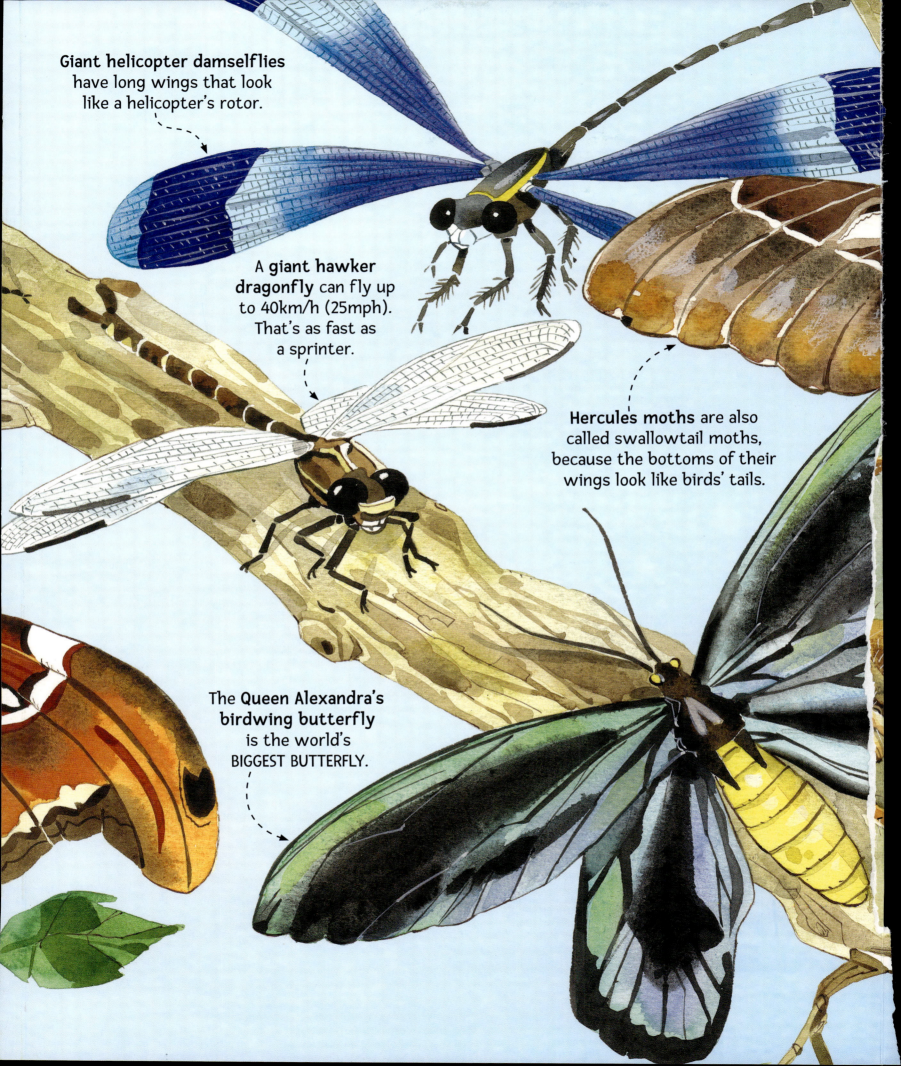

Giant helicopter damselflies have long wings that look like a helicopter's rotor.

A **giant hawker dragonfly** can fly up to 40km/h (25mph). That's as fast as a sprinter.

Hercules moths are also called swallowtail moths, because the bottoms of their wings look like birds' tails.

The **Queen Alexandra's birdwing butterfly** is the world's BIGGEST BUTTERFLY.

Golden silk orb-weaving spiders weave huge webs that can be as tall as a two-floor house.

Peruvian yellowleg centipedes can have around 40 legs. Their front legs are filled with poison to kill prey.

A **giant African black millipede** has up to 250 legs – the most of any bug.

The **goliath birdeater spider** is one of the largest spiders in the world.

When a birdeater is frightened, it shakes poisonous hairs off its back.

It kills big bugs, mice and lizards with its big fangs. But it hardly ever eats birds.

Hidden bugs

Some bugs look like other things, which makes them difficult to spot. This hides them from attackers, and also helps them catch prey.

Groups of **thorn bugs** cling to branches. Their spiky green bodies are similar to thorns on a stem.

A **Chan's megastick** can be as long as an adult's arm. It stays hidden in trees as it looks like a twig.

Bird dropping spiders' bodies are covered in white silk. Other creatures think the spiders are droppings, so they don't get eaten.

It's hard to see this **giant leaf insect** on a leafy green plant.

They also hide under leaves.

Leaf insects' bodies, legs and heads look like leaves.

The **dead leaf butterfly's** wings are brown and crinkled, like dead leaves.

Assassin bugs hunt other bugs. An assassin will stab a bug with its sharp mouthparts, then suck out the insides.

If they're attacked, they spit a poisonous liquid in their attacker's eyes.

Giant water bugs eat bugs and small animals, including frogs and turtles. They grab prey with their strong front legs, then inject them with poison.

A **giant vinegaroon** seizes beetles or spiders, then uses its fearsome jaws to crush them.

Deadliest bugs

Armed with sharp jaws, painful stings or deadly poison, some bugs are very harmful to other bugs, animals or humans.

In real life, the tsetse fly is only this big.

It's shown bigger here so you can see it more clearly.

Tsetse fly
Female tsetse flies bite people and animals to suck out the blood. They pass on deadly diseases.

Black widow spider
Black widows bite their prey and inject a deadly poison at the same time.

The non-flying dorylus is actually very small. It's shown bigger here so you can see what it looks like.

Non-flying dorylus actual size

Flying dorylus

Dorylus ant
Dorylus ants devour any creature that gets in their way.

Saddleback caterpillar
Saddleback caterpillars' bright green and red markings warn other animals not to eat them.

Lonomia caterpillar
Lonomia caterpillars are covered in extremely poisonous hairs.

Giant water bug
Water bugs live underwater. They have sharp mouthparts that they use to stab prey.

The fattail scorpion's sting is in the end of its tail.

Fattail scorpion
The fattail scorpion is the world's MOST DANGEROUS SCORPION. The poison in its sting can kill a person.

Assassin bug
Assassin bugs hide under dead leaves, then jump out and attack their prey.

Giant Asian hornet
Giant Asian hornets attack big bugs and nests of bees. A hornet can kill 40 bees in a minute.

Bullet ant
Of all insects, bullet ants have the MOST PAINFUL STING. They will attack intruders to their nests.

The acid is like vinegar, which is how the vinegaroon got its name.

Giant vinegaroon
If a giant vinegaroon is attacked, it will spray stinging acid from its tail.

Fangs

Sydney funnel spider
The Sydney funnel spider has big fangs to inject poison into its prey.

Giant tarantula hawk wasp
Giant hawk wasps hunt some of the biggest spiders in the world, including the goliath birdeater spider.

Brazilian wandering spider
Brazilian wandering spiders hide in plants, then jump out and bite their prey.

Big beetles

Beetles are some of the biggest and heaviest bugs. They eat natural waste, including rotting wood and fruit, and even dung.

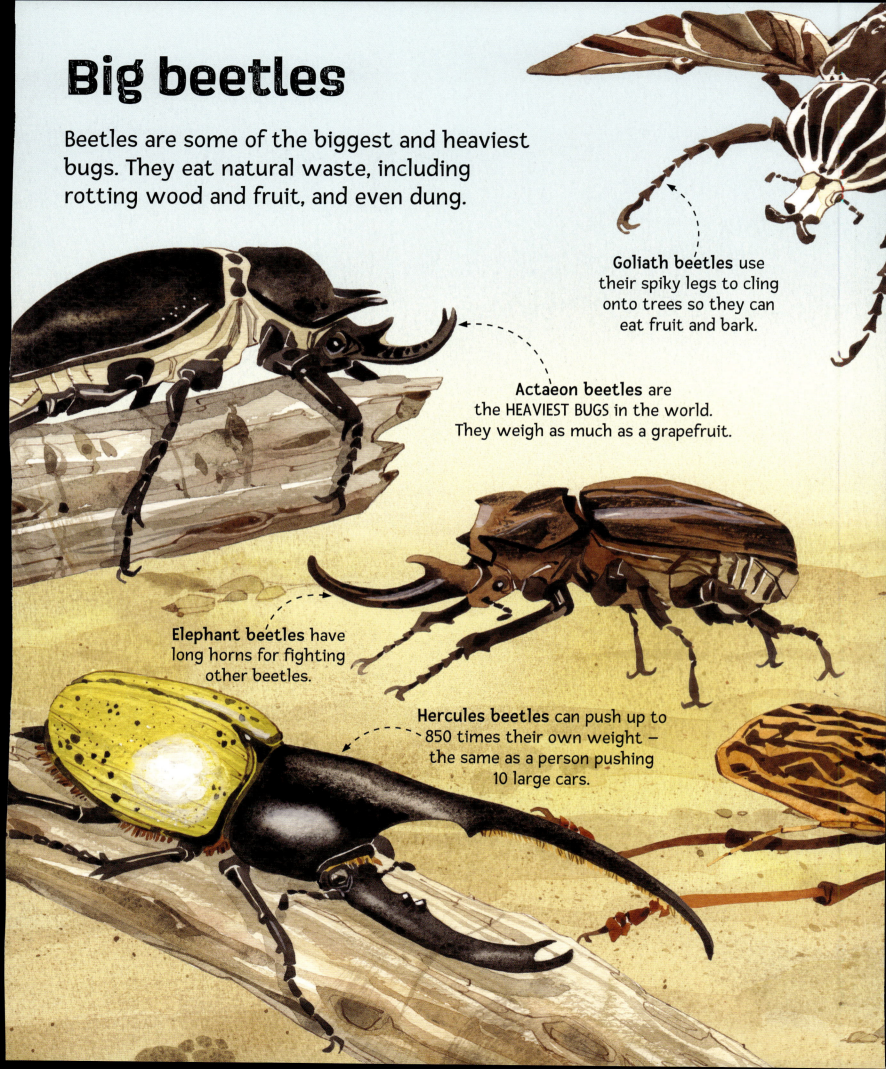

Goliath beetles use their spiky legs to cling onto trees so they can eat fruit and bark.

Actaeon beetles are the HEAVIEST BUGS in the world. They weigh as much as a grapefruit.

Elephant beetles have long horns for fighting other beetles.

Hercules beetles can push up to 850 times their own weight — the same as a person pushing 10 large cars.

Monarch butterflies fly for weeks every winter to escape the harsh cold. They land on trees to rest every few days.

When they're together, the butterflies' bright, patterned wings confuse attackers.

Termite nests are home to thousands of termites. Workers patrol the nest, repairing any damage.

Every year honey bees look for a new place to build a nest. They gather in big swarms, like this, before they set off.

A swarm of locusts devours an enormous amount of food per day – as much as 450 million people would eat in the same period.

Gigantic groups

Some bugs live together in huge groups, or form big swarms. Some of these bugs are very small, so they're shown larger here than they really are.

Desert locust
Group size: up to 40 billion
After it rains, locusts form massive swarms to feed and find mates.

The bugs' actual sizes are shown here.

The queen termite has a big, white body.

Mound building termite
Group size: over 1 million
Termites build very tall nests – over 9m (30ft) high.

Fire ant
Group size: up to 500,000
Fire ants live in huge nests. The queen lays 1,000 eggs per day.

They collect pollen from flowers in tiny pouches on their legs.

Honey bee
Group size: up to 10,000
Bees use pollen to feed their young.

Actual sizes

Yellowjacket wasp
Group size: 5,000
Yellowjackets make nests from chewed-up wood.

Actual size

Monarch butterfly
Group size: over 100 million
Monarch butterflies fly from North America to Mexico every winter.

Mosquito
Group size: over 1 million
Swarms of mosquitos fly over rivers and lakes. Females have a nasty bite.

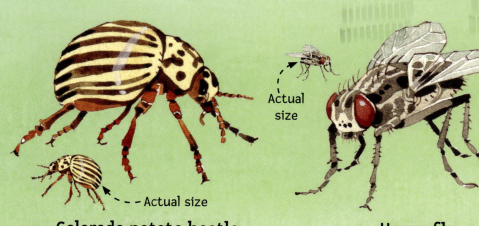

Colorado potato beetle
Group size: up to 30,000
Colorado beetles can devour whole potato or tomato crops.
— Actual size

House fly
Group size: up to 1,000
Big swarms of house flies feed on rotting waste.
Actual size

Asian lady beetle
Group size: thousands
Asian lady beetles flock to warm, sunny surfaces.
Actual size

Lake flies are very small. A swarm looks like this.

Male lake flies use their feathery antennae (feelers) to find females.

Lake fly
Group size: many millions
Lake fly swarms are so big, they look like thick, black clouds.

Empress cicada
Group size: Hundreds of millions
Cicadas swarm to find a mate. Males create a loud "song" — as loud as a jumbo jet's engine — to attract females.

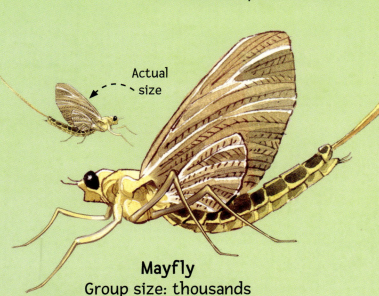

Actual size

Mayfly
Group size: thousands
Mayfly young live underwater. They come to the surface to turn into adults and find mates.

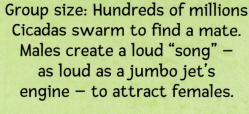

Purple crow butterfly
Group size: over 11,000
Purple crow butterflies gather in massive groups to find warmer weather in the winter.

Strongest, heaviest, longest...

Here are some more bugs, both big and small...

Horseflies fly FASTER than any other bug. They can reach 144km/h (90mph) – the speed of a fast car.

Jewel beetles are the world's LONGEST-LIVED BUG. The oldest jewel beetle lived for 47 years.

Jewel beetles' bodies are covered in tiny scales that sparkle in the sunlight.

The **mole cricket** uses its shovel-like feet to dig long 6m (20ft) burrows.

The **dung beetle** is the STRONGEST BUG. It can push up to 1,141 times its own weight – like a person lifting six double-decker buses.

The **Madagascan hawk moth** feeds on a flower called the comet orchid.

It sucks nectar from the orchid's nectar tube with its 28cm (11in) long tongue.

Dung beetles roll balls of dung for their young to eat.

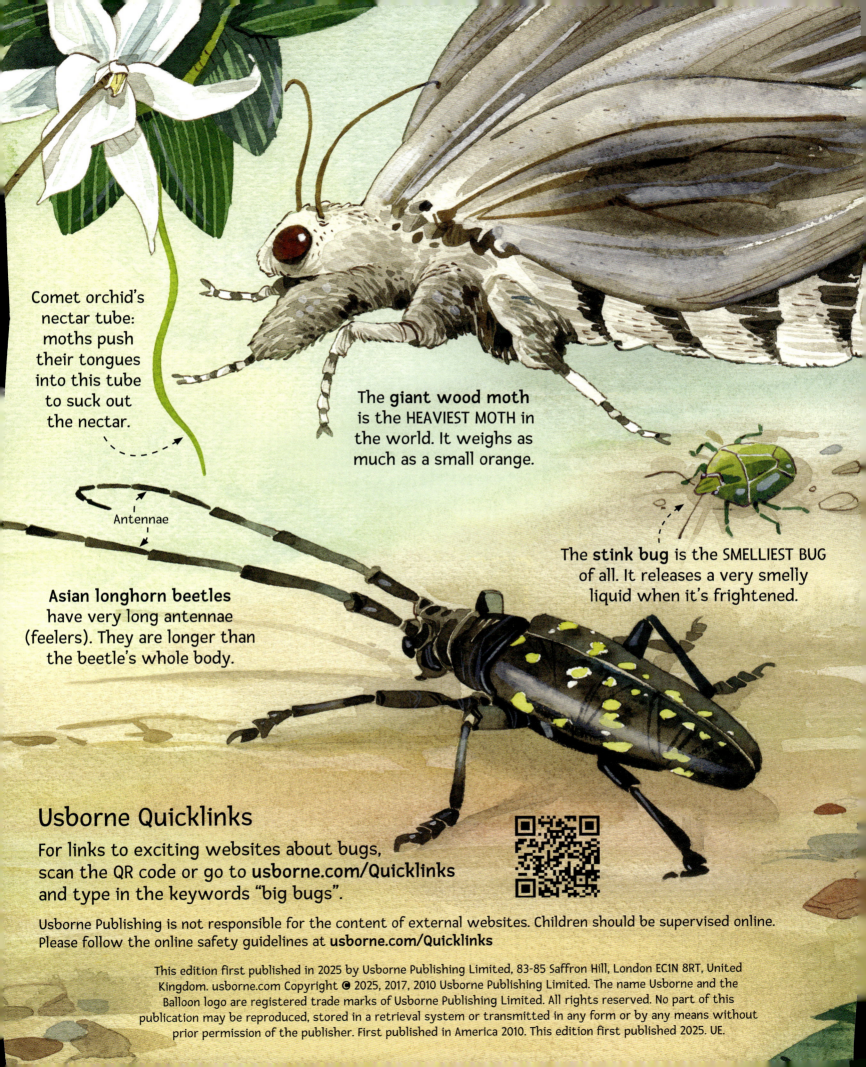

Comet orchid's nectar tube: moths push their tongues into this tube to suck out the nectar.

The **giant wood moth** is the HEAVIEST MOTH in the world. It weighs as much as a small orange.

The **stink bug** is the SMELLIEST BUG of all. It releases a very smelly liquid when it's frightened.

Antennae

Asian longhorn beetles have very long antennae (feelers). They are longer than the beetle's whole body.

Usborne Quicklinks

For links to exciting websites about bugs, scan the QR code or go to usborne.com/Quicklinks and type in the keywords "big bugs".

Usborne Publishing is not responsible for the content of external websites. Children should be supervised online. Please follow the online safety guidelines at usborne.com/Quicklinks

This edition first published in 2025 by Usborne Publishing Limited, 83-85 Saffron Hill, London EC1N 8RT, United Kingdom. usborne.com Copyright © 2025, 2017, 2010 Usborne Publishing Limited. The name Usborne and the Balloon logo are registered trade marks of Usborne Publishing Limited. All rights reserved. No part of this publication may be reproduced, stored in a retrieval system or transmitted in any form or by any means without prior permission of the publisher. First published in America 2010. This edition first published 2025. UE.